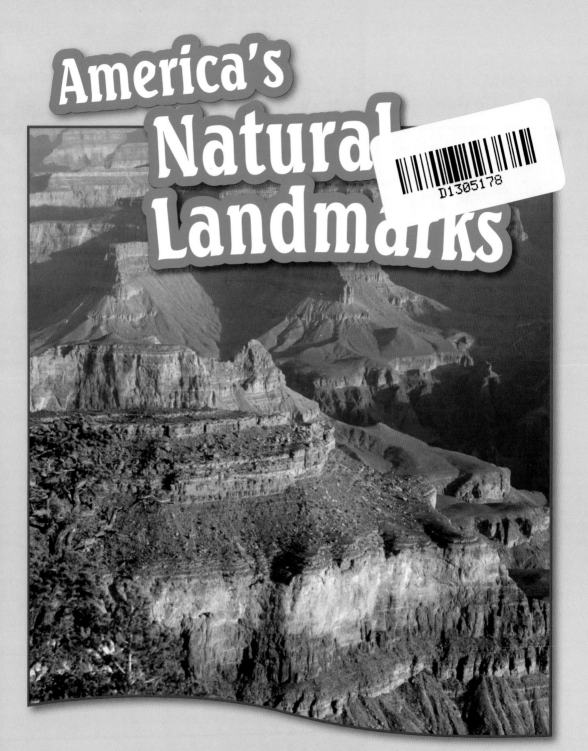

America's
Natural
Landmarks

Jennifer Overend Prior, Ph.D.

D1305178

Consultant

Caryn Williams, M.S.Ed.
Madison County Schools
Huntsville, AL

Image Credits: pp.2–3 Johner Images/age fotostock;
pp.12–13 David Noble/nobleIMAGES/Alamy; pp.20–21
Chris Howes/Wild Places Photography/Alamy; p.6 John Elk
III/Alamy; p.9 (bottom) John Hyde/Alaska Stock/Alamy; p.28
(top) Pat Canova/Alamy; p.27 (top) Ron Niebrugge/Alamy;
p.29 (top) Paul A. Souders/Corbis; p.19 (top) Paul Seigle/
Flickr; p.10 (bottom) Allard Schager/Flickr/Getty Images;
pp.22–23 Barcroft Media/Getty Images; pp.6–7 (background)
G. Brad Lewis/Aurora/Getty Images; pp.16–17 (both) Lowell
Georgia/National Geographic/Getty Images; p.7 (top)
tankbmb/iStock; p.13 John Burcham/National Geographic
Creative; p.20 DanitaDelimont.com/Newscom; p.17 (top)
Karen Uhlenhuth KRT/Newscom; pp.8–9 (background)
Michael DeYoung/Newscom; p.24 (top) Niagara Falls Public
Library; p.26 Tim Sloan/AFP/Newscom; p.15 (all) Lionel
Bret/Science Source; pp.18–19 (background) Wikimedia
Commons; all other images from Shutterstock.

Library of Congress Cataloging-in-Publication Data

Prior, Jennifer Overend, 1963-
    America's natural landmarks / Jennifer Overend Prior, Ph.D.
        pages cm
    Includes index.
    ISBN 978-1-4333-7371-8 (pbk.)
    ISBN 978-1-4807-5157-6 (ebook)
    1. Natural areas—United States—Juvenile literature. I. Title.
    QH76.P744 2014
    508.73—dc23
                                                    2014010586

Teacher Created Materials

5301 Oceanus Drive
Huntington Beach, CA 92649-1030
http://www.tcmpub.com

ISBN 978-1-4333-7371-8

© 2015 Teacher Created Materials, Inc.

Table of Contents

Natural Landmarks

Landmarks are special places. They are big and easy to see. They can help people find their way. If you see a landmark, it may help you figure out where you are in your town, state, or country. Landmarks are each important in their own way.

Some landmarks are made by people. Others are created by nature. These are called *natural landmarks*. There are many natural landmarks in America. There are **canyons** and waterfalls. A large hole can even be a natural landmark! They remind us of the awesome power of nature. And they show us the beauty that America has to offer.

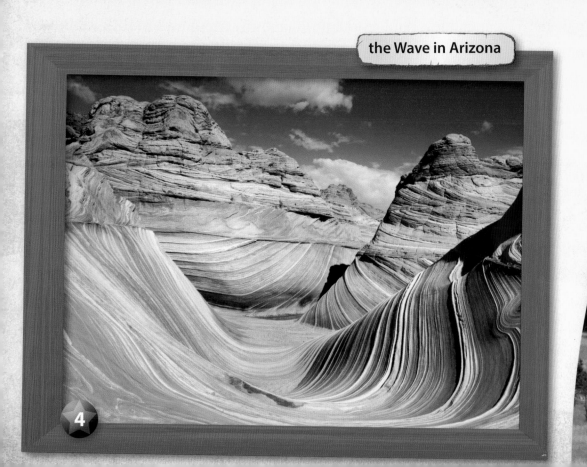

the Wave in Arizona

Local Landmarks

Do you have any landmarks in your hometown? Maybe there is a funny-shaped tree by your favorite park. Or maybe there is a big lake by your school. How do your local landmarks help you?

Devils Tower National Park in Wyoming

Mesa Arch in Canyonlands National Park in Utah

Western Landmarks

Kilauea (kee-lou-EY-ah) is a natural landmark. It is a volcano on the Big Island of Hawaii (huh-WAHY-ee). A volcano is a mountain that has a hole in the top or the side. Sometimes, **lava**, ash, and rocks will shoot out of the hole. This is called an *eruption* (ih-RUHP-shuhn). An eruption can happen at any time. And it can happen very fast!

Kilauea has had 61 eruptions! Even today, lava keeps flowing out of the volcano. The lava will harden and dry. This makes new land. It makes the Big Island of Hawaii even bigger. There are many volcanoes in Hawaii. Kilauea is the youngest and the most active. In fact, it is one of the most active volcanoes in the world!

Pele

Kilauea is the home of Pele (PEH-ley). Pele is the mythical Hawaiian goddess of fire. Hawaiians leave fruit, fish, and flowers by the volcano for her. They do this to thank her for making their island bigger.

Kilauea

Lava flows from Kilauea.

Glacier (GLEY-sher) Bay is in Alaska. It has mountains and beaches. It also has lots of glaciers. Its glaciers are a natural landmark. A glacier is a very large area of ice that moves slowly down a slope or **valley**.

At Glacier Bay, you can take a boat to see the glaciers. Sometimes, large blocks of ice will break. They crash into the water of the bay. It is an amazing sight to see! But you have to stay at least two miles away from the glaciers. This is to keep you safe from the falling ice.

A tip of a glacier breaks off and falls into the water.

Whale Watching

You can also see whales in Glacier Bay. Humpback whales travel from Hawaii to Alaska. They like to eat there during the summer.

Sequoia (si-KWOI-uh) National Forest is in northern California. It is home to the world's largest trees. They are called *giant sequoia trees*. They are evergreen trees. This means that their leaves stay green all year long. The trees grow high in the mountains. They are so big that they drink about 500 gallons of water each day. You would have to drink about 4,000 bottles of water to drink as much as one of these trees! The giant sequoias live to be about 3,000 years old. And their bark is three feet thick!

You can even walk through a giant sequoia tree. You can also drive through one of these giant trees in a car! It is called *Tunnel Log*.

giant sequoia tree

Tunnel Log in Sequoia National Park

General Sherman

The General Sherman tree is the largest living tree in the world. It is 2,100 years old and is 275 feet tall. It is named after a man who was a leader in the Union Army during the Civil War.

When most people think of natural landmarks, they think of the Grand Canyon. It is a very large, deep valley in Arizona. This is a hot and dry part of the country. But snow falls in the Grand Canyon, too. This is because it is so high.

The Grand Canyon was made over millions of years by **erosion** (ih-ROH-zhuhn). This is when water or wind wear away at rocks or dirt. The Colorado River runs through the canyon. Over time, the river and wind wear away at the rocks. This made the deep canyon that we see today.

You can stand on the rim, or edge, of the canyon. You can also hike down to the bottom. Millions of people visit the Grand Canyon each year.

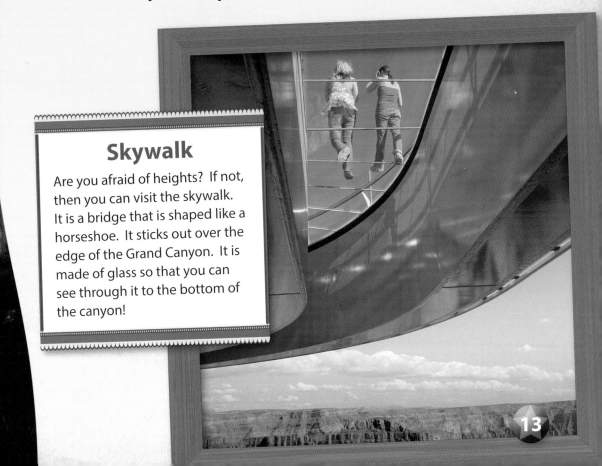

Skywalk

Are you afraid of heights? If not, then you can visit the skywalk. It is a bridge that is shaped like a horseshoe. It sticks out over the edge of the Grand Canyon. It is made of glass so that you can see through it to the bottom of the canyon!

Meteor Crater is in the northern part of Arizona. A crater is a large hole that is made when a meteorite hits Earth.

Meteor Crater was formed thousands of years ago. A meteorite fell from space and hit Earth. It made a big hole in the ground that is over two miles wide. It is very deep, too.

For many years, **scientists** did not know what made the crater. But after years of study, they learned that it was a meteorite. Over time, a lake filled the crater. Years later, the lake dried up. The area is now very dry. This is why the crater is still so large. Many people visit the crater every year.

A meteor crashed here 49,000 years ago.

This shows how a meteorite makes a crater.

Meteor, Meteroid or Meteorite?

A rock in space is called a *meteroid*. It is called a *meteorite* if it hits Earth's surface. When a meteroid enters Earth's atmosphere, it starts to burn. This burning flash of light that we see is called a *meteor*.

15

A quarry is a place where people dig for stone. But one quarry in Utah is different. There, scientists dig for dinosaur bones! It is called the Dinosaur National **Monument**. Dinosaurs were reptiles that lived on Earth millions of years ago. Reptiles are living things like snakes and lizards. They are cold-blooded and lay eggs. Their bodies are covered with thin plates called *scales*.

Many dinosaur bones have been found at the quarry. Most of the bones come from dinosaurs that ate meat. Scientists think that a nearby river washed the bones down to the quarry long ago. Over time, some of the bones were buried.

Visitors watch as scientists chisel dinosaur bones out of the rocks.

I Touched a Dinosaur!

Today, you can see and touch some of the dinosaur bones at the quarry. Can you imagine touching a dinosaur bone that is 150 million years old?

A scientist outlines a dinosaur in the rock.

A Midwestern Landmark

Marengo (muh-RANG-go) Cave is in Indiana. A brother and sister found it in 1883. They were 11 and 15 years old. Soon, the cave was open to visitors.

The cave is filled with interesting rock formations, or shapes. One kind is called a *stalactite* (stuh-LAK-tahyt). These look like rock spikes hanging from the ceiling of the cave. They are made by water dripping from the top of the cave. The water carries parts of the rocks from the top of the cave as it drips. Over time, this makes stalactites.

The cave stays cool in the summer and winter. It is home to different animals, such as mice and bats. Many people visit the cave each year.

Make a Wish!

Have you ever seen an upside-down wishing well? There is a ceiling at Marengo Cave that is so sticky with mud that you can throw coins at it and they will stay! It is a **tradition** to make a wish and throw a penny to the ceiling.

stalactite

Southern Landmarks

Devil's **Sinkhole** is a very deep hole in the ground in Texas. If you look into the large hole, you will not be able to see the bottom. Visitors are not allowed to go into the sinkhole. Only scientists can go inside. Scientists think that American Indians used to take rocks from the sinkhole long ago. They would use them to make tools.

The sinkhole is also home to millions of bats in the summer. Every night, the bats fly out of the sinkhole. They leave to look for food. They return before sunlight. Many people come to see the bats fly in and out of the sinkhole.

Bats and Birds

The number of bats that live in Devil's Sinkhole varies. It depends on the time of year. Sometimes, there are about 30,000 bats. Other times, there can be about one million bats! But they are not the only animals living in the sinkhole. Birds and bugs live down there, too.

Manatee Springs is in Florida. A spring is a place where water flows out of the ground. The water is usually warm because Earth is warm deep underground. There are many springs in the world.

In Manatee Springs, bright blue water flows out of the ground day and night. Manatees are big animals that eat plants and swim in the sea. The spring got its name because manatees spend the winter months there. The sea is cold and manatees cannot stay in cold water for long. They come to the springs in Florida because they like the warm water.

This area is fun for people, too. It is a great place to swim and see the manatees. People also like to go there for picnics.

Gentle Giants

Manatees are sometimes called *sea cows*. They move slowly and eat plants and algae.

A Northeastern Landmark

Niagara (nahy-AG-ruh) Falls is made up of three large waterfalls. Two of the falls are in New York. The other one is in Canada. Waterfalls are created when rivers fall off cliffs. Niagara Falls became a **state park** in 1885. It is the oldest state park in America.

Where Did the Water Go?

On May 29, 1848, the water stopped flowing over the falls. Ice had blocked the water from flowing over the falls. The water was blocked for a few hours. People could walk out on top of the falls!

The falls are fun to visit, but they are useful, too. The water travels over the falls very quickly. Over time, people learned how to turn the water's power into **electricity**. They did this by building a dam downstream. This is a wall that stops or slows water. The water then runs through pipes. There, the water spins large blades. The blades are attached to an engine. It turns the water's movement into electricity. This power helps light homes and schools.

Preserving Our Landmarks

The National Park Service helps preserve, or save, landmarks in America. It protects natural sites and helps keep them safe and clean. This lets everyone enjoy them. We need to do our part, too. Each state has places that are special. We can help them stay there for many more years. This way, they will always be a part of our country.

Find out if there are any natural landmarks near you. Ask your family to visit one of them. While you are there, be respectful of the land and nature. Visiting these places will help you learn more about America.

President George W. Bush talks to park rangers at Everglades National Park in 2001.

NATIONAL PARK SERVICE

A park ranger leads a tour of Exit Glacier in Alaska.

Visit It!

There are many natural landmarks all over our country. Which one is closest to you? Find a natural landmark that is near your home and that you would like to visit. Plan a trip to see it!

A mother and son kayak at Manatee Springs.

A family views Niagara Falls.

This girl plans her trip to visit a natural landmark.

Glossary

canyons—deep valleys with steep rock sides and often has a stream or river flowing through it

electricity—a form of energy that is carried through wires and is used to operate lights and machines

erosion—the process of breaking something down by the action of water, wind, or glacial ice

glacier—a very large area of ice that moves slowly down a slope

lava—hot liquid rock above Earth's surface

manatee—a large animal that lives in warm waters and eats plants

monument—a building, statue, or place that honors a person or an event

scientists—people who are trained in science and do scientific research

sinkhole—a low area or hole in the ground that is formed when soil and rocks are removed by flowing water

state park—an area of land that is owned and protected by the state because of its natural beauty and importance

tradition—a way of thinking or doing something that has been done by a particular group for a long time

valley—an area of low land between hills or mountains

Index

Your Turn!

My Favorite

You learned about many different natural landmarks in this book. Which one was your favorite? Why? Create a travel brochure to advertise your favorite natural landmark.

America's Natural Landmarks

Many of America's natural landmarks have become famous. People like to visit them because they are unique and beautiful. They remind us of the power of nature. It is important to preserve these places so that everyone can enjoy them.

NATIONAL PARK SERVICE

Department of the Interior

Geography

Lexile® 580L

ISBN 978-1-4333-7371-8

50000

9 781433 373718

TCM 18371

T3-CCA-155